T0194978

ONE WORD ONE YEAR FAITH JOURNEY

A 12 Month Guided Journal Experience to Grow in Faith with a One Word Focus

Michelle Robblee

WESTBOW PRESS®
A DIVISION OF THOMAS NELSON
& ZONDERVAN

WestBow Press books may be ordered through booksellers or by contacting:

WestBow Press
A Division of Thomas Nelson & Zondervan
1663 Liberty Drive
Bloomington, IN 47403
www.westbowpress.com
1 (866) 928-1240

ISBN: 978-1-9736-9045-0 (sc)
ISBN: 978-1-9736-9046-7 (e)

Print information available on the last page.

WestBow Press rev. date: 4/28/2020

Dedicated to my parents,
Ray and Patricia Mooney.

Thank you for showing me how to live a life for Him.
Thank you for your endless encouragement, support and love.
I love you.

CONTENTS

ONE WORD FAITH BASED JOURNEY

Whether you've selected a 'Word for the Year' before, or you're brand new to the concept, welcome! This **One Word One Year Faith Journey** is Christian based. This book is a guided journal filled with faith prompts and activities to help you grow in your Christian walk by being intentional with your One Word. The first section of this book walks you through choosing your One Word for the year. Once you've selected your One Word, the monthly journal prompts will encourage, challenge, guide, assist and lead you into taking the next steps in your faith journey. These prompts are designed to change your outlook, shift your mindset, nourish your soul and allow God to work through every area of your life. Are you up for the adventure of trusting Him more fully? Are you ready for a year focused on drawing nearer to Him?

This 12 month guided journal is not a New Year's resolution goal-setting workbook, but instead a guide to direct you closer to God by having a One Word focus. This intentional focus powered by the Spirit's leading will allow you to make lasting spiritual, mental and even physical changes in your life. This is a yearlong study that can be started anytime. Typically most begin this process every January, but don't let timing stop you from starting this journey. No matter what month of the year, pick up this guide and start right at the beginning.

The One Word you choose for the year doesn't hold any power of course, it's just a simple word. The Almighty God, or the Trinity, (Father, Son, Holy Spirit) is the one who holds all the power and He's already at work in you, no matter what word you choose. He has the power to not only lead you to choose One Word for the year, but to work through your One Word and redirect you, encourage you, strengthen you, grow you and draw you closer to Him. He does the work. You make the decision to follow, trust and submit to Him as He works in your life.

Choosing One Word to intentionally focus on throughout the year, provides a constant redirect to remember your intentions. A resolution usually leads to frustration and failure. However, focusing on One Word doesn't show you've failed, but continues to 'show up' throughout your days and causes you to take notice. Each time you come across your One Word, whether in print, speech or sound, you will find yourself stopping and noticing. That pause will cause you to think, re-adjust, take action and be drawn to God. You can use your One Word as a constant reminder to direct yourself to Him and your One Word intentions all year long, every day, every hour, minute by minute.

You decide how much energy and effort to put into this. You can journal every day or once a month. You can write out thoughts for every prompt, or just for the prompts you want. You can participate in all the activities or just a few. You can hold monthly gatherings with a small group and complete this journey with friends, or privately work through it yourself. You decide.

HOW TO USE THIS JOURNAL

Begin this journey by reading through the section titled, **Choosing Your One Word** and complete the suggested prompts and activities. Write out your thoughts and ideas right in this book. After choosing and committing to One Word for the year, begin the **Monthly Prompts** starting with Month 1. Work through each prompt and write out your thoughts. This can be done daily, completing a little at a time, weekly or even once or twice a month. Do what works for you. If there isn't enough space to write out all you want to record, use an additional blank journal alongside this book.

In addition to the Monthly Prompts, each month you'll be asked to add a new scripture to your **One Word Scripture Collection.** The scriptures you collect should relate to your One Word and encourage you. These can be hand-written on index cards or kept digitally on your phone or tablet. At the end of the year, you will have collected scripture truths that will encourage you in your One Word. Maybe you will even challenge yourself to memorize them?

At the end of each month are **Optional Creative Activities** to complete with your One Word. Creating with your One Word can be very beneficial. Not only does it provide a creative outlet to apply your One Word to, but it gives you various art and objects to place in your home or workplace. When you see those objects, you'll immediately be redirected to your One Word intentions. At the back of this book on page 141, you will find a section titled, **More Creative Art Activities**. These additional activities are to inspire you to bring creative life and art to your One Word. These can also be used as small group activities if you're completing this journey with others.

In addition to creative activities, you will also be given the opportunity to write out your thanksgivings to God in the **Give Thanks Challenge**. By recording things you are thankful for, your mind shifts from focusing on yourself to noticing and thanking God. In a gratitude-seeking state of mind, you are reminded that there is always something to be thankful for. The very act of giving thanks and writing it down, confirms that God is good, faithful and trustworthy. There are approximately 84 blank lines each month to write out your gratitude to God. If you write down 84 thanksgivings for every month of the year (or about 3 a day), you will have over 1000 at the end of the year! Challenge yourself to give thanks to the Lord during this entire journey. Giving thanks can be for the big thanksgivings, miracles, gifts and answered prayers in your life…AND for the small, tiny little things God has you noticing. Record them all!

Optional Tracking Charts are also included every month. These can be used however you see fit with your One Word intentions. You may want to track a new monthly routine or habit, by filling in the dated bubbles as you complete a chosen activity. The charts could also be used to stop a negative habit, by filling in the bubbles every time you are successful. Tracking charts give you a visual of your intentions and successes. These charts can encourage and motivate you as you see your progress over time.

Each month continue working through that month's **Monthly Prompts, Creative Activities, One Word Scripture Collection, Give Thanks Challenge and Optional Tracking Charts.** As you work through these prompts and activities, allow your chosen One Word and its intentions to permeate into all you do, think and say. Notice changes in your heart, mind and soul. Notice how a simple One Word and the power of the Spirit can you lead you to Him over and over again.

I pray that this journey will grow your faith, mold your heart and draw you nearer and closer to God like never before. A year with your One Word will pass by quickly and soon you'll come to the end of this 12 month journey.

I pray that this is not the end, but another opportunity to choose a new One Word to continue your growth with Him.

If you are interested in completing this Journey with the support of a small group, please turn to the section titled **Small Group One Word Faith Journey** on page 139 for helpful tips and suggestions.

CHOOSING YOUR WORD

You might already have your word picked out for the year, or maybe a word has already found you? Yes, sometimes that happens and you know right away. Or maybe you have no idea what your word should be or where to even begin? Let me reassure you that you can't choose a wrong word. God works through anything and anyone and most-definitely through any word. There is nothing He can't work with or through or in. The process of choosing a word should not be stressful. There is no right or wrong word for you. By working through these prompts and exercises, certain words may be repeated and may start to peak your interest. You might have words that jump off the page and cause you to take notice, or words that keep reappearing over and over in your responses. Be on the lookout.

Even if you already think you have your word chosen, continue to work through these start-up exercises and prompts. You might be surprised what comes to the surface? Maybe you'll find a completely different word or maybe you'll reconfirm the same word you had chosen all along?

Talk With God:

The best place to start this journey is in prayer and conversation with God. Feel free to write out your prayers or spend this time in prayer on your knees. Either way, no matter where you are in your faith journey, talk with God. Some of the following prayer prompts might be too much for where you are in your faith, that's okay. Just keep reading through the prompts and using this time to talk with God. Be assured that God always hears your prayers.

First, glorify God. Praise Him and thank Him for this past year and His faithfulness. Thank Him that you are alive, which means He still has good plans for you here on earth. Thank Him that He never leaves you or forsakes you, never stops loving you, never forgets you or gives up on you. He is always with you no matter what! Praise God!

Next, dedicate this year to Him. Tell God that you want Him to be the #1 priority in your life. That you're ready to live your year with Him being in charge, leading the way. You want Him guiding, strengthening, helping and leading you. You want to trust that His plans for your life are good and you want to bring Him glory in every aspect of your life. Ask Him to change your heart from your desires to His desires. Ask Him to help you trust Him. Ask Him to draw you nearer and nearer to Him.

Begin to talk to God about the upcoming challenges and concerns you foresee in the year ahead. Tell Him your fears and apprehensions. Tell Him your worries, stresses and frustrations. Tell Him your burdens and anxieties. Lay it all out before Him and tell Him what is holding you back from releasing your cares to Him. What are you holding onto? Why?

Sit in silence. Ask God to direct your thoughts to Him and help you be attentive to any words and phrases He may be bringing to your mind. Be still. Rest in His presence. Wait on Him. Record the words that come into your mind.

Journal These Questions:

Thinking ahead to the end of this year, where would you like to be:

Mentally-

Spiritually-

Physically-

Relationally-

Professionally-

Financially-

Other Areas-

What are your goals, dreams and aspirations for the year ahead?

What do you feel God is allowing you to see in yourself, that needs attention, work, focus or change?

What do you need to do to move forward into a healthy mindset and mental freedom?

Word Bank:

The following list of words is not exhaustive, but a sample selection of words to help you journal and explain your thinking. Use this list as a tool and know that your chosen One Word may or may not be on this list.

Word Bank:

abide	content	flow	kind	prayerful
adore	consistent	focus	learn	prepared
action	connect	fortitude	leap	present
allow	courage	forward	less	progress
appreciate	creativity	finish	light	purpose
arise	crusade	freedom	lighthearted	push
aspire	curious	friend	listen	quiet
awake	deep	generous	look	rebuild
balance	delight	go (let go)	love	reflect
battle	devoted	grace	minimize	release
be	different	grateful	momentum	relationship
believe	diligence	gratitude	more	relentless
better	discipline	growth	move	resilient
bless	discover	happy	notice	resolve
blessing	embrace	healthy	nurture	rest
brave	empower	heart	obedience	reveal
breathe	encourage	honor	open	rise
begin	endure	hope	opportunity	savor
calm	engage	ignite	optimism	seek
care	enjoy	illuminate	pace	self-control
centered	enough	imagine	pause	serenity
celebrate	evolve	improve	passion	shift
certainly	explore	inspire	peace	shine
challenge	faith	integrity	persevere	silence
change	fearless	intentional	persistence	silent
cherish	no fear	intimate	play	sit
clarity	filled	joy	possibility	simplify
commit	flourish	journey	power	simplicity

silence	strength	trust	vigilant	worship
slow	strong	truth	vitality	yield
soul	surrender	unafraid	warrior	
space	thrive	unleash	well	
stewardship	transform	unstoppable	whole	
still (be still)	today	uplift	wisdom	

Brain Dump:

Brainstorm words and phrases for each of the following questions.

*With my God and Savior I want to...

*In my spiritual walk, I want to...

*With my daily living, I want to...

*With my spouse/significant other, I want to...

*With my family and/or children, I want to...

*With my friends, I want to…

*With my church, I want to…

*With my job, career, business, I want to…

*With my health and well-being, I want to…

*Within my home, I want to…

*In my hobbies and interests, I want to…

*In managing finances, I want to…

*New things I'd like to do this year…

*Things I'd like to NOT do this year…

*I feel God may be calling me to…

*In other areas/situations/problems/happenings, I want to…

Narrow Down the One Word Possibilities:

Go back and look through the words and phrases you wrote down on the Brain Dump questions. Highlight the words or themes that appear more than once and the ones that are capturing your interest. Make a new list of each of those highlighted words. Read through the Word Bank list again, circling words or highlighting words that you used in your prompts or words that are speaking to you.

Which words are jumping out at you? Which words do you keep coming back to? Could one of these words help and guide you through multiple areas in your life? Sit with your new list of words and pray over them. Allow the Spirit's leading to help you choose One Word. This process could happen very quickly, or take days of mulling over in your head. Take the time you need to choose One Word for the year.

Once you have your One Word, write it in big letters right here on this page. Commit to give this One Word a full year. Circle it, star it and draw arrows pointing to it. Write the date next to it. You now have your One Word for the Year. Let's get started on this journey.

MONTH 1 PROMPTS

What led you to choose your One Word?

What are your intentions and expectations for this One Word to help guide your year?

<u>Intentions:</u>

<u>Expectations:</u>

Listen and journal what you feel God may be asking you to do this year. How does it relate to your One Word?

<u>Definitions</u> of my One Word:

<u>Synonyms</u> of my One Word:

<u>Antonyms</u> of my One Word:

Are there Biblical references to your One Word?

Are there characters, stories, parables or prophesies in the Bible that relate to your One Word? Look up those passages, read the scriptures and journal what speaks to you within those references.

Look up scriptures in the Bible where your One Word appears. Use an online concordance to help. Write out the verses that encourage you. If your One Word is not in scripture, try looking for scriptures using synonyms for your One Word or other scriptures that relate. If interested, find quotes that speak to you about your One Word as well. (When using quotes, remember that they are not God's words or His truths.)

Optional Monthly Trackers

These monthly trackers are for your own use. Is there a habit you're trying to break or trying to adopt? Write the activity name or habit on the tracker and fill in the bubble each day you are successful. Trackers are a visual tool to see and celebrate attempts and successes. Trackers are encouraging and motivating as you visually see your growth. If trackers are frustrating to you, don't use them.

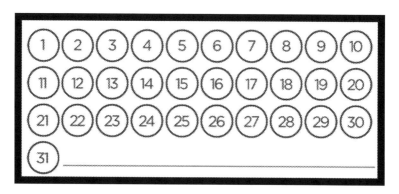

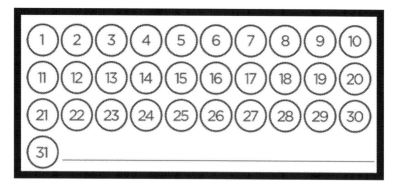

One Word Scripture Collection:

Each month you'll be asked to choose one scripture that encourages you in your One Word. Write this scripture on an index card, punch a hole in it and place the card on a metal book ring. This allows you to carry the card around with you and continue to add a new scripture to your ring each month. If you'd rather keep the scriptures on your phone or computer, that's fine too. Make this scripture your monthly focus. Place it around your home. Learn this verse and try to memorize it. Speak this verse aloud, pray it over yourself and allow the power of God's truths to soak into your soul every day.

Write your monthly scripture in the box.

Optional Creative Activities:

Add your One Word to the cover or inside cover of this book. Use a permanent marker, letter stickers or any other art to personalize your journal. If using a blank notebook alongside this book, decorate the cover of your notebook with your One Word.

Purposely read Christian books about your One Word. Highlight or make notes each time your One Word appears. Journal thoughts and meditate over what speaks to you. Keep a list of the books you read all year long. Use page 143, **Books Read** page to record the titles. You could also keep a record of podcasts, lectures or sermon notes and record how they relate to your One Word.

If interested, see page 141 for **More Creative Art Activities.**

Give Thanks Challenge:

**Rejoice always, pray without ceasing, give
thanks in all circumstances: for this is the
will of God in Christ Jesus for you.
1 Thessalonians 5: 16-18**

The Give Thanks Challenge is an exercise designed to train your mind to give thanks in all things. The challenge is to write down your daily thanksgivings to God. When you choose to thank Him for the little things that you don't always notice, the big things you clearly see AND the hard things, your heart and mindset begin to change. Challenge yourself to write out your thanksgivings to God and see what He can do through this. When you set out to give Him thanks, you'll notice that there is always something to be thankful for. The very act of giving thanks and writing it down confirms that our God is good and faithful.

There are 84 blank lines each month to write out your thanksgivings to God. (That's about 3 blessings a day.) If you keep up with this every month you'll have over 1000 recorded blessings at the end of the year! Challenge yourself to give thanks to the Lord during this entire journey. You can do this!

1.

2.

3.

4.

5.

6.

7.

8.

9.

10.

11.

12.

13.

14.

15.

16.

17.

18.

19.

20.

21.

22.

23.

24.

25.

26.

27.

28.

29.

30.

31.

32.

33.

34.

35.

36.

37.

38.

39.

40.

41.

42.

43.

44.

45.

46.

47.

48.

49.

50.

51.

52.

53.

54.

55.

56.

57.

58.

59.

60.

61.

62.

63.

64.

65.

66.

67.

68.

69.

70.

71.

72.

73.

74.

75.

76.

77.

78.

79.

80.

81.

82.

83.

84.

MONTH 2 PROMPTS

Write facts and feelings you're experiencing with your One Word.

What is your One Word an invitation to do or not to do? Will you accept the invitation?

How do you sense the Holy Spirit directing you in your One Word?

What is the Spirit…

-whispering to you?

-showing you?

-guiding you to do?

-teaching you?

Is God asking you to do something specific with your One Word for Him?

For yourself?

For others?

Will you respond in obedience?

Choose one small thing that you feel called to do or practice this month. Intentionally practice or do this item for the month of February.

Maybe follow through with a Monthly Tracker to keep yourself accountable?

Continue to pray over your One Word—listen, watch, reflect.

Optional Monthly Trackers

These monthly trackers are for your own use. Are you feeling led to follow through on a small practice or habit? Write the activity name or habit on each tracker and fill in the bubble each day you are successful throughout the month. Remember, the goal is not perfection but growth. Trackers are a visual record of you trying a new thing. Celebrate your success and progress.

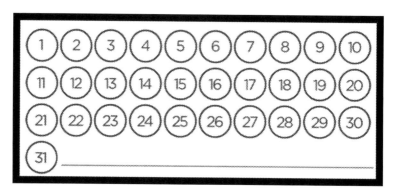

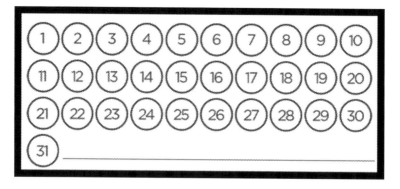

One Word Scripture Collection:

Are you collecting your scriptures on note cards? If so, add another notecard with your new scripture on it. Are you collecting scriptures on your phone? Add a new one for this month. Make this scripture your focus. Remember to place it around your home and learn it. Pray it over yourself and allow the scripture to encourage you in this journey.

Write out your scripture for the month in the box.

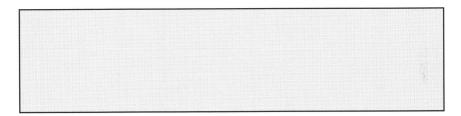

Optional Creative Activities:

Create visual art with your One Word and frame it. Place your One Word art in a prime spot to remind yourself of your intentions. Create a colorful background using watercolors, acrylics, oil paints or mixed media. Add your One Word to the art using creative lettering, stamps, or make graphics on your phone or computer.

If interested, see page 141 for **More Creative Art Activities.**

Give Thanks Challenge:

**Praise the LORD! Oh give thanks to the LORD, for
he is good, for his steadfast love endures forever!
Psalm 105:3**

God is good and faithful. His love is true and it never runs out. The very act of giving thanks to Him and writing it down confirms and provides proof that He is good and faithful and He loves us. Don't skip this challenge. Three thanksgivings recorded each day is all you need. You can do this!

85.

86.

87.

88.

89.

90.

91.

92.

93.

94.

95.

96.

97.

98.

99.

100.

101.

102.

103.

104.

105.

106.

107.

108.

109.

110.

111.

112.

113.

114.

115.

116.

18 |

117.

118.

119.

120.

121.

122.

123.

124.

125.

126.

127.

128.

129.

130.

131.

132.

133.

134.

135.

136.

137.

138.

139.

140.

141.

142.

143.

144.

145.

146.

147.

148.

149.

150.

151.

152.

153.

154.

20 |

155.

156.

157.

158.

159.

160.

161.

162.

163.

164.

165.

166.

167.

168.

MONTH 3 PROMPTS

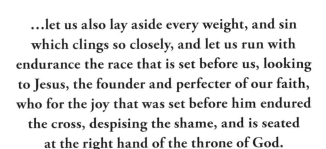

**…let us also lay aside every weight, and sin
which clings so closely, and let us run with
endurance the race that is set before us, looking
to Jesus, the founder and perfecter of our faith,
who for the joy that was set before him endured
the cross, despising the shame, and is seated
at the right hand of the throne of God.
Hebrews 12:1b-2**

What is weighing you down? Make a list of your 'weights'.

How does your One Word relate to these things?

As you live out the life that God has placed before you, where are you looking for help?

What is keeping you from looking to Jesus? How can looking to Jesus become automatic in your life? Journal your thoughts on this.

LENT

If your One Word One Year Faith Journey began in January, Month 3 is the month of March. Typically, this is when the Christian's Lenten season begins. Lent is the 40 days (not counting Sundays) before Easter. The purpose of Lent is to reflect on the sacrifice of Christ. It is often associated with repentance, soul searching, reflection and re-dedicating your life to follow Him. Many Christians choose to fast or abstain from something as a reminder of Christ's sacrifice and love. Some choose to add a good practice or service during the 40 days to focus on Christ's life and sacrifice.

As you reflect on the darkness of living in sin and the light of your Savior and God, how can you practice Lent to lead you to walking in the light?

How can your One Word draw you closer to Jesus as you remember His life, death and resurrection this month?

Will you be 'giving up' or 'adding in' something for the Lenten season? How does this practice relate to your One Word? Make a plan of action. Use a Monthly Tracker to visually keep you accountable.

Optional Monthly Trackers

These monthly trackers are for your own use. Are you feeling led to follow through on a fast from something or an added practice for the Lenten season? The 40 day tracker can be used for Lent. Write the activity name or practice on the tracker and fill in the bubble each day you complete your chosen practice.

Lent Tracker

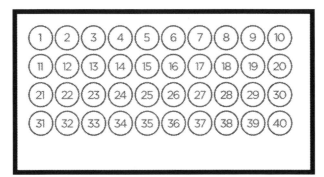

Monthly Trackers

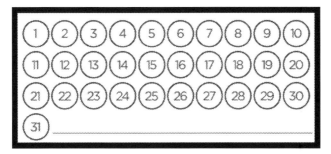

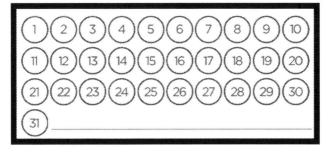

One Word Scripture Collection:

Choose another scripture to add to your One Word Scripture Collection. Make this scripture your monthly focus. Continue to review all of your scriptures and practice memorizing them. Remind yourself to recite these truths during the day. Are you allowing yourself to believe these verses and let them encourage you in your faith? Pray for the desire to fully believe and trust in God's Holy Word.

Write out your scripture for the month in the box.

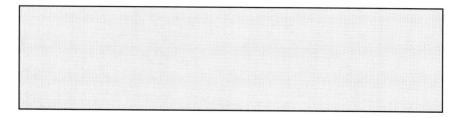

Optional Creative Activities:

Make a purpose-filled vision board. Choose a canvas board, poster board, bulletin board or even the next page in this journal. This could also be done digitally on your phone or computer. If using magazines, cut out pictures, words and images of what your One Word means and represents to you. If not using magazines, print out computer graphics to use. Adhere items to your board and display it in a place where you'll see it often. View your board daily to remind you of your vision and intentions with your One Word. May viewing this board encourage and inspire you to keep on persevering on this journey.

If doing this in a small group. Share completed vision boards with the group. See page 141 for **More Creative Art Activities.**

VISION BOARD

Give Thanks Challenge:

Oh give thanks to the LORD, for he is good;
for his steadfast love endures forever.
1 Chronicles 16:34

The Lord is so good! His love never changes and never runs out. Don't let your praise and thankfulness to Him run dry. Continue on this challenge of writing down all that you are thankful for. Let this practice become a daily habit.

169.

170.

171.

172.

173.

174.

175.

176.

177.

178.

179.

180.

181.

182.

183.

184.

185.

185.

186.

187.

188.

189.

190.

191.

192.

193.

194.

195.

196.

197.

198.

199.

200.

201.

202.

203.

204.

205.

206.

207.

208.

209.

210.

211.

212.

213.

214.

215.

216.

217.

218.

219.

220.

221.

222.

223.

224.

225.

226.

227.

228.

229.

230.

231.

232.

233.

234.

235.

236.

237.

238.

239.

240.

241.

242.

243.

244.

245.

246.

247.

248.

249.

250.

251.

252.

MONTH 4 PROMPTS

**Seek the LORD and his strength;
seek his presence continually!
1 Chronicles 16:11**

Where do you see your One Word in your life right now?

Are you being 'tripped up' by your One Word? How? Explain.

What do you need to 'let go of' to truly embrace your One Word?

How is your One Word leading you closer to God? Or how can it? Will you let it? What do you need to do to make this happen?

If you participated in a Lenten experience in the last 40 days. Reflect on that and journal your thoughts.

Write a manifesto related to your One Word.

A manifesto is a statement and/or declaration where you share your intentions and motives.

Start your manifesto by finishing these statements:

I believe.....

I know this to be true.....

I want to.....

I will be intentional about....

Rewrite these statements into full sentences that clearly state your One Word intentions for the year.

My Manifesto

Copy your manifesto and display in a place where you will read it and remember. Place a copy near or on your vision board too.

Optional Monthly Trackers

These monthly trackers are for your own use. Are you feeling led to follow through on a practice or habit? Write the activity name or habit on each tracker and fill in the bubble each day you are successful. Trackers are a visual tool to see and celebrate attempts and successes. These are supposed to be encouraging and motivating as you track progress visually. Celebrate your success and progress.

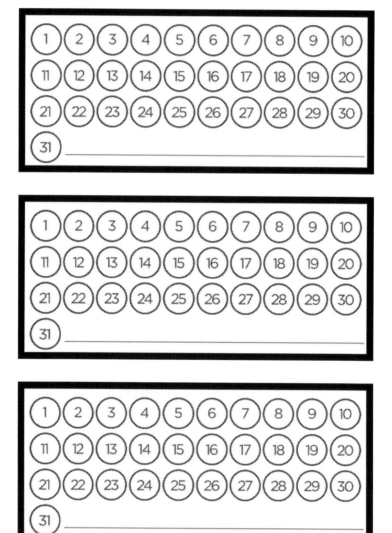

One Word Scripture Collection:

Add another scripture to your One Word Scripture Collection. Remember to choose scriptures that relate to or encourage you in your One Word and your intentions. Speak these verses aloud and allow the power of God's truths to encourage you.

Write out your scripture for the month in the box.

Optional Creative Activities:

Spend some time with music. Whether it's your favorite artist, songs from the radio or hymns and praise songs, find songs that have your One Word in them. Write out your favorite phrases and or verses. Journal why you resonate with a song, phrase or chorus. Sing your songs to the Lord. Meditate on your songs as you praise God with singing. Write out the song lyrics and display them in your home. May this activity bring you encouragement and a reminder to lift up your voice to the Lord.

If doing this activity with a small group, share the songs with each other and create a playlist that contains each person's chosen song.

If interested, see page 141 for **More Creative Art Activities.**

SONG JOURNALING

Give Thanks Challenge:

**Oh come, let us sing to the LORD; let us make a
joyful noise to the rock of our salvation! Let us
come into his presence with thanksgiving; let us
make a joyful noise to him with songs of praise!
Psalm 95:1-2**

Do you ever sing out your praises to Him? Go ahead, SING! Thank Him for music and the gift of singing. Continue on this challenge of writing down your thanksgivings to the Lord. Nothing is too small to give Him thanks.

253.

254.

255.

256.

257.

258.

259.

260.

261.

262.

263.

264.

265.

266.

267.

268.

269.

270.

271.

272.

273.

274.

275.

276.

277.

278.

279.

280.

281.

282.

283.

284.

285.

285.

286.

287.

288.

289.

290.

291.

292.

293.

294.

295.

296.

297.

298.

299.

300.

301.

302.

303.

304.

305.

306.

307.

308.

309.

310.

311.

312.

313.

314.

315.

316.

317.

318.

319.

320.

321.

322.

323.

324.

325.

326.

327.

328.

329.

330.

331.

332.

333.

334.

335.

336.

MONTH 5 PROMPTS

Celebrations: List three things you're enjoying about your One Word.

1.

2.

3.

Surprises: List three things that have surprised you about your One Word.

1.

2.

3.

Struggles: List three things that are challenging you about your One Word.

1.

2.

3.

Reflect on your celebrations, surprises and struggles. Can you see growth, movement, God at work in you?

Look back over the struggles and challenges you listed. Think about a current trial you are facing this month. Can you faithfully thank God in advance for what He is doing and how He is in control?

Ask Him to provide assurance and deep peace as you boldly trust Him.

**Do not be anxious about anything, but in everything by prayer and supplication with thanksgiving let your requests be made known to God. And the peace of God, which surpasses all understanding, will guard your hearts and your minds in Christ Jesus.
Philippians 4:6-7**

Journal a prayer of thanksgiving using these prompts.
Thank God for:

His provisions:

His comfort:

His protection:

His faithfulness:

His perfect timing:

His hand in all things:

His power:

His strength working in you:

His guidance:

His plan to use you for His glory:

His love for you:

Optional Monthly Trackers

These monthly trackers are for your own use. Are you feeling led to follow through on a practice or habit? Write the activity name or habit on each tracker and fill in the bubble each day you are successful.

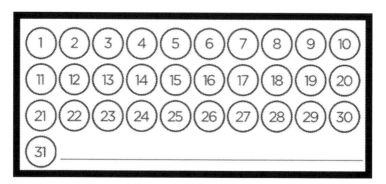

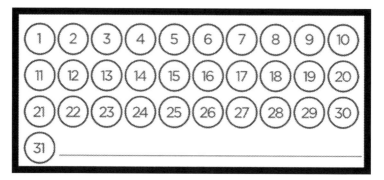

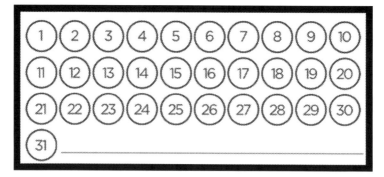

One Word Scripture Collection:

Time to add another scripture to your collection. Are you able to recall and recite these verses throughout your day? Are these scriptures reminding you of your One Word intentions? Challenge yourself to memorize these and say them to yourself. A challenging day, filled with His truths, brings about an indescribable peace and calmness to your soul. Practice this. Journal what you notice from adding scriptures to your days.

Write out your scripture for the month in the box.

```



```

Optional Creative Activities:

This is your invitation to be in silence with God. Go outside, sit, be still and breathe. Take time to calm yourself and listen. Wait on the Spirit. Journal anything that comes to your mind. Thank God for His revelations. Begin a time of prayer. Praise God for who He is, all He has created, all He has done for you, all He has revealed to you. After you praise and glorify Him, begin to pray over yourself and your One Word. Ask God to reveal new insights for you.

While outside, gather an object, such as a flat rock, leaf or a branch. Write/paint/color your One Word on this living object. Bring this object inside and let it be a reminder to get outside, be still and listen for Him.

If doing this activity with a small group, ask each member to do this activity on their own and bring in a rock to decorate together.

If interested, see page 141 for **More Creative Art Activities.**

Be Still and Listen Journaling:

Give Thanks Challenge:

**And let the peace of Christ rule in your
hearts, to which indeed you were called
in one body. And be thankful.
Colossians 3:15**

Take your thankful list outside as you complete your Creative Activity this month. Give thanks to God for all you see, breathe, feel and touch. Continue on this challenge of writing down the big and small things that you are thankful for.

337.

338.

339.

340.

341.

342.

343.

344.

345.

346.

347.

348.

349.

50 |

350.

351.

352.

353.

354.

355.

356.

357.

358.

359.

360.

361.

362.

363.

364.

365.

366.

367.

368.

369.

370.

371.

372.

373.

374.

375.

376.

377.

378.

379.

380.

381.

382.

383.

384.

385.

385.

386.

387.

388.

389.

390.

391.

392.

393.

394.

395.

396.

397.

398.

399.

400.

401.

402.

403.

404.

405.

406.

407.

408.

409.

410.

411.

412.

413.

414.

415.

416.

417.

418.

419.

420.

MONTH 6 PROMPTS

<u>Halfway Point—Take Inventory</u>

You're halfway through the year! Way to go! Look back over your journaling from the beginning of this journal to now.

What do you notice?

Are you seeing any spiritual growth taking place? Journal what you notice.

Do you see areas that you have conquered, mastered or matured in?

Do you see areas that you haven't touched on or worked on yet? Make note of these.

Self-evaluate how you're doing with your:

-Monthly Prompts

-Scripture Collection and Memorizing

-Give Thanks Challenge

-Monthly Trackers

-Optional Creative Activities

-Remembering your One Word intentions

Reflect on how you're feeling with your One Word.

Does your One Word still make sense to you? Does it still feel 'right'?

Have 'companion words' come up? Record these words and why you think they're appearing.

Describe your One Word experience so far? Are you surprised where this One Word has taken you or not taken you?

**Commit your way to the Lord; trust
in him, and he will act.
Psalm 36:12**

Do you need to re-dedicate yourself to this journey? Have you gotten off track and lost momentum? If so, write out a prayer to God asking for direction, perseverance and a strong desire to continue on this faith journey of seeking Him and trusting Him with your life.

After reviewing your One Word work so far, what intentions did you notice that still need work? Has God been nudging you for obedience in a certain area with your One Word?

What specifically do you feel called to do? Write that goal or healthy practice down and break it into one or two small steps to work on this month. Ask God for direction, strength and leading. Commit yourself to Him and begin to daily take the steps needed to be obedient. Use the prompts and monthly tracker to assist you. Share your commitment with a friend for accountability.

List Spiritual Goal/Healthy Practice:

Break Goal Into Small Steps:

Choose one or two small steps to make a concentrated effort towards your goal. Use the monthly tracker to keep you accountable.

Optional Monthly Trackers:

Are you practicing a spiritual goal or a healthy practice this month? Write the activity name on each tracker and fill in the bubble each day you are successful. Trackers are a great visual to look back at your progress and celebrate your initiative to try a new habit or activity. The goal of a tracker is not perfection, but progress and growth.

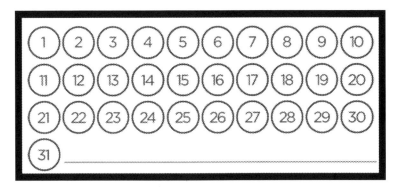

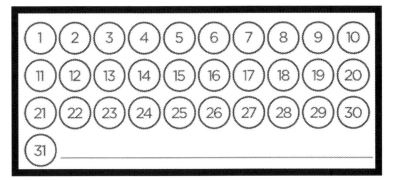

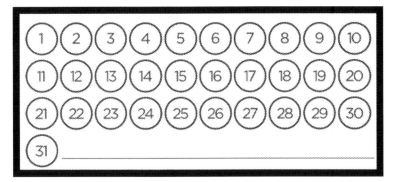

One Word Scripture Collection:

Add another scripture to your Scripture Collection that will encourage you in your chosen goal. Pray this scripture for yourself and make this scripture your monthly focus. When you start to fall off track of your intentions, reach for your Scripture Collection and pray for God's strength to help you persevere. See this month's Optional Creative Activities with lots of ideas to get creative with your scriptures.

Write out your scripture for the month in the box.

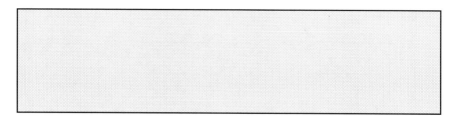

Optional Creative Activities:

You are at the halfway mark with 6 scriptures collected. Display these verses around your home, workplace, car, etc. Find creative ways to get these scriptures in front of you. Recite them daily and pray them over yourself. Here's some ideas to try:

- Write scripture on white boards or chalkboards.
- Spell out scripture on letter boards, bulletin boards or other displays.
- Tape scripture cards on the refrigerator and the dashboard of your car.
- Place scripture cards in plastic resealable sandwich bags and they'll stick to your shower walls.
- Use dry erase markers and write scriptures on your mirrors.
- Write scriptures on sticky notes and place around computer or treadmill.
- Create art with your scriptures and display.

— ake your scripture cards when you go for a walk. Practice memorizing the verses as you walk.

If interested, see page 141 for **More Creative Art Activities.**

Give Thanks Challenge:

**Let them thank the LORD for his steadfast
love, for his wondrous works to the children
of man! For he satisfies the longing soul, and
the hungry soul he fills with good things.
Psalm 107:8-9**

This month you will reach the halfway mark of the year with 500 recorded gratitudes. Yes! Commit to continuing this challenge all the way to 1000. You can do it!

421.

422.

423.

424.

425.

426.

427.

428.

429.

430.

431.

432.

433.

434.

435.

436.

437.

438.

439.

440.

441.

442.

443.

444.

445.

446.

447.

448.

449.

450.

451.

452.

453.

454.

455.

456.

457.

458.

459.

460.

461.

462.

463.

464.

465.

466.

467.

468.

469.

470.

471.

472.

473.

474.

475.

476.

477.

478.

479.

480.

481.

482.

483.

484.

485.

486.

487.

488.

489.

490.

491.

492.

493.

494.

495.

496.

497.

498.

499.

500.

501.

502.

503.

504.

MONTH 7 PROMPTS

Did you take on the Month 6 Challenge Activity? If so, take some time to reflect and journal.

Did you feel God's leading to persevere in a specific calling or activity?

Were you obedient?

Did you notice changes?

Breakthroughs?

Disappointments?

Growth?

Continue working on your goal and record your next small steps to work on this month.

Focus on your One Word and 'freedom' this month.

**Now the Lord is the Spirit, and where the
Spirit of the Lord is, there is freedom.
2 Corinthians 3:17**

**For freedom Christ has set us free;
stand firm therefore, and do not submit
again to a yoke of slavery.
Galatians 5:1**

Journal the following prompts:

Are you feeling burdened and weighted instead of free?

What are you submitting to that is not godly?

What do you need to 'stand firm' in and not submit to?

How can you stand firm and release your weighty burdens (even if your circumstances don't change)?

Read each of the following spiritual practices that bring freedom to a Christ follower. Ask yourself if you're neglecting these practices and journal your thoughts.

Scripture/Bible Reading

Praising God

Scripture Memorizing

Grateful/Thankful Record

Serving Others

Prayer

Meditation

Bible Study

Sharing the Gospel

Which of these practices are you struggling with that could be made into an action plan for growth? What small thing could be done to become a daily habit that would allow you more freedom, peace and joy? Journal your thoughts and make a plan. Use the monthly trackers to help you stay focused and accountable.

Optional Monthly Trackers

What area did you choose from the Christian practices list to commit to? Use a monthly tracker to follow through on your intentions. Choose a small activity and track your progress. Fill in the bubble each day you are successful. Trackers are a great visual tool to see and celebrate your attempts and successes.

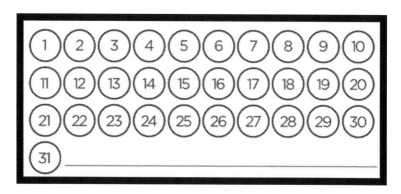

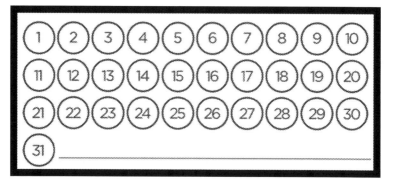

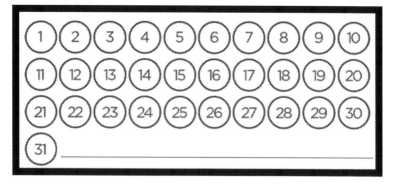

One Word Scripture Collection:

Choose another scripture to add to your One Word Scripture Collection. Learn this verse and memorize it. Daily review your scripture collection and speak the verses aloud, pray the scriptures to God and allow His truths to calm and encourage you. May the strength of God equip you for your day.

Write out your scripture for the month in the box.

Optional Creative Activities:

Make bookmarks with your One Word on them. Create watercolor art on card stock paper. Add your One Word to each bookmark and one of your verses on the back. Tie on a ribbon or tassel.

Challenge yourself to read a Christian book that relates to your One Word this month. Journal insights that speak to you. Have you read and recorded any books on page 143, Books Read? Take the time to read a Christian book and take notes and reflect when you see your One Word in print. Add your completed book to your 'Books Read' on page 143.

If doing this activity with a small group, ask each member to bring their book to the group meeting. Have them share a book synopsis and a few key points they wrote down to remember.

If interested, see page 141 for **More Creative Art One Word Activities.**

Give Thanks Challenge:

**Continue steadfastly in prayer, being
watchful in it with thanksgiving.
Colossians 4:2**

You've passed the halfway mark! There's no quitting now. Continue on this challenge of writing down your thankfulness to God. Are your eyes always on the lookout for God's blessings? Be watchful AND thankful.

505.

506.

507.

508.

509.

510.

511.

512.

513.

514.

515.

516.

517.

518.

519.

520.

521.

522.

523.

524.

525.

526.

527.

528.

529.

530.

531.

532.

533.

534.

535.

536.

537.

538.

539.

540.

541.

542.

543.

544.

545.

546.

547.

548.

549.

550.

551.

552.

553.

554.

555.

556.

557.

558.

559.

560.

561.

562.

563.

564.

565.

566.

567.

568.

569.

570.

571.

572.

573.

574.

575.

576.

577.

578.

579.

580.

581.

582.

583.

584.

585.

586.

587.

588.

MONTH 8 PROMPTS

**And I pray that the sharing of your faith may
become effective for the full knowledge of every
good thing that is in us for the sake of Christ.
Philemon 1:6**

How does your One Word relate to you sharing the gospel with others?

Think about the people in your life who do not know Jesus. Write their names down.

Pray over each person on your list and ask God if you are being called to share Jesus with someone on this list

Listen and wait on the Spirit. Pray over each name again, this time putting their name into this scripture from **Acts 26:18.**

Open_____'s eyes, so that he/she may turn from darkness to light and from the power of Satan to God, that he/she may receive forgiveness of sins and a place among those who are sanctified by faith in Jesus.

Has God called you to share Jesus with a specific person? If so, will you be obedient? How? Continue to write out your prayers to God asking Him to encourage you to share your faith with others. Is there an action step you can take to be obedient to God's command to share the gospel?

Is this exercise of praying Acts 26:18 something that God is calling you to do daily? Weekly? Monthly? Set up a tracker to pray daily over a specific person this month. Ask God how He would like you to witness to, care for or love on each person on your list. Ask God to give you opportunities to connect with these people and bless them with the gift of Jesus.

Circle back to the beginning of this journey. Reread your responses on pages xviii-xix and focus in on how your One Word can be applied to these areas. Maybe your responses have changed since the beginning of your journey? Do you have new thoughts, ideas and/or goals you'd like to meet? Record your thinking under each area listed.

Mentally:

Physically:

Spiritually:

Relationally-

Professionally-

Financially-

Other Areas-

Spend time in prayer and ask the Spirit to show you what areas need to be focused on at this point in your journey. Record what is brought to your mind.

Choose one or two areas to focus on and record what small steps or habits could be made to make a conscious effort of growth this month. Consider using a Monthly Tracker to help you stay accountable.

Optional Monthly Trackers

Set up a tracker to pray over a non-believer or a small goal to make progress in a needed area in your life. Commit yourself to making an effort and seeing what God does with your faithfulness. Write the activity name or practice on each tracker and fill in the bubble each day you are successful.

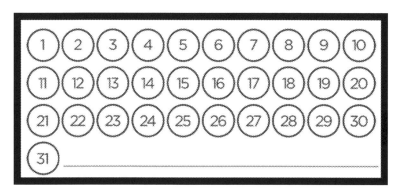

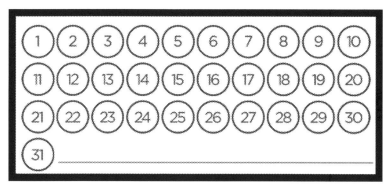

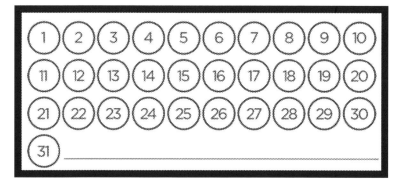

One Word Scripture Collection:

Choose another scripture to add to your One Word Scripture Collection. Make this scripture your monthly focus. Place it around your home. Learn this verse and try to memorize it. Daily review your scripture collection and speak the verses aloud, pray these scriptures over yourself and allow the power of God's truths to soak into your soul, encourage you and equip you for the day.

Write out your scripture for the month in the box.

Optional Creative Activities:

Try this activity on a day where you might have a bit more flexibility with your schedule. Set your phone timer (or other timer you might have—Smart watch, Fitbit, etc.) to go off every hour throughout the day. Each time the timer rings, redirect your thoughts to God. Spend a minute or two praying and listening to Him. Ask Him to flood your thoughts with His love and show you what your focus should be in whatever you're currently in the middle of. Reflect and ask yourself if you're being intentional with your One Word in this particular moment of the day. Are you doing things in alignment to your One Word intentions? Are you being counterproductive and doing things to lead you away from your One Word intentions? Record your observations.

*Try this activity a few times this month and see if it brings you a renewed passion to be intentional with your One Word.

If interested, see page 141 for **More Creative Art Activities.**

TIMER JOURNALING

Give Thanks Challenge:

**The LORD is my strength and my shield; in
him my heart trusts, and I am helped; my heart
exults, and with my song I give thanks to him.
Psalm 28:7**

He is your helper. You can trust Him and give Him thanks. He is your
strength to continue on this journey, don't stop! Write down your gratitudes
to Him and allow Him to strengthen you.

589.

590.

591.

592.

593.

594.

595.

596.

597.

598.

599.

600.

601.

602.

603.

604.

605.

606.

607.

608.

609.

610.

611.

612.

613.

614.

615.

616.

617.

618.

619.

620.

621.

622.

623.

624.

625.

626.

627.

628.

629.

630.

631.

632.

633.

634.

635.

636.

637.

638.

639.

640.

641.

642.

643.

644.

645.

646.

647.

648.

649.

650.

651.

652.

653.

654.

655.

656.

657.

658.

659.

660.

661.

662.

663.

664.

665.

666.

667.

668.

669.

670.

671.

672.

MONTH 9 PROMPTS

You're in the final season of this journey. Time to recommit and focus in on some of the toughest questions yet! While working through these prompts, spend time in prayer asking God to bring to your mind what He wants you to see, feel and do. Take time to answer these questions with an open honest heart that can bring a new awareness and additional healing and growth in your spiritual journey. Will you submit to Him and follow His guidance?

**Commit your way to the Lord; trust
in him, and he will act.
Psalm 37:5**

Have you neglected your One Word and its purpose and intentions to lead you to Him? Yes or No? Why or why not?

Have you allowed yourself to fully invest in making God the #1 priority of your life? Why or why not?

Are you allowing your One Word and the Spirit's leading to make needed and positive changes in your life and relationships? How?

How are your recent changes, habits and/or decisions good and pleasing, honoring God's plans for your life?

What habits and/or decisions are causing you to be stagnant and unmoving in your faith, pointing you in the opposite direction of God?

What is God telling you to let go of?

What is God saying to embrace?

Are you resisting changes and God's call for you? Why?

Where do you feel God's leading for you in this new season?

Do you need to change an attitude, response or behavior?

Recommit yourself to your intentions. Rewrite, re-read and pray out your scriptures from your One Word Scripture Collection. Journal your thoughts to God and ask Him for a renewed desire to seek Him and trust Him with His plans for your life.

Optional Monthly Trackers

Did you uncover a needed attitude or behavior change from this month's prompts? Can you choose a small step and commit to tracking your desires and intentions to make changes? Write the small practice step on a tracker and fill in the bubble each day you are successful. Thank God for the desire to persevere in growing closer to Him.

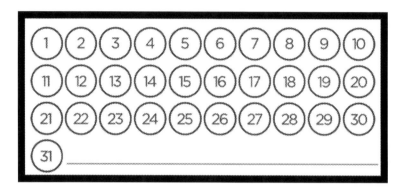

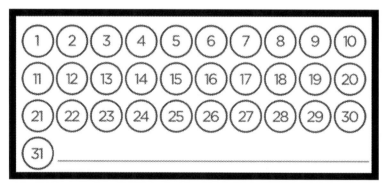

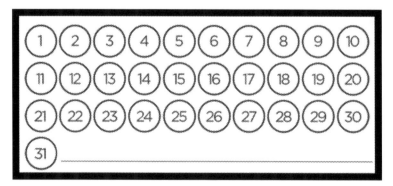

One Word Scripture Collection:

Add another scripture (or two? Or more?) to your One Word Scripture Collection. Why stop at one? Remember to review your collection daily. Make time each day to say these verses aloud and proclaim them over yourself. Submit yourself to Him and ask Him to grow your love for His Holy Word.

Write out your scripture for the month in the box.

Optional Creative Activities:

This month try embracing Task Oriented Praying. Make a list of everyday tasks/chores you do during the day. (For example: make bed, walk dog, make breakfast, brush teeth, drive car, etc.) Assign one thing to pray for while you complete that specific task. For instance: while you make your bed, pray for your spouse. While you walk your dog, pray for your neighbors. While you make breakfast, pray for your health. See if you can get into a habit of automatically praying specific things while completing your daily tasks. Make a list of your tasks and what you can pray for while you complete them. (Use chart on the next page to do this.) Challenge yourself to try this for a month. Maybe you'll want to have little reminder cards around your home to help you keep this habit or use a Monthly Tracker to keep you accountable?

If interested, see page 141 for **More Creative Art Activities.**

Everyday Tasks	What to Pray

Give Thanks Challenge:

**Enter his gates with thanksgiving, and his courts
with praise! Give thanks to him; bless his name!
Psalm 100:4**

Give thanks wherever you are and wherever you go. Even if you don't have your journal with you to write your thanksgivings down, give thanks! Make this a natural habit that pours out of you no matter what! Praise Him!

673.

674.

675.

676.

677.

678.

679.

680.

681.

682.

683.

684.

685.

686.

687.

688.

689.

690.

691.

692.

693.

694.

695.

696.

697.

698.

699.

700.

701.

702.

703.

704.

705.

706.

707.

708.

709.

710.

711.

712.

713.

714.

715.

716.

717.

718.

719.

720.

721.

722.

723.

724.

725.

726.

727.

728.

729.

730.

731.

732.

733.

734.

735.

736.

737.

738.

739.

740.

741.

742.

743.

744.

745.

746.

747.

748.

749.

750.

751.

752.

753.

754.

755.

756.

MONTH 10 PROMPTS

It's the final 3 months of the year. Look back 6 months ago at the manifesto you wrote in Month 4 on page 33.

What progress have you made?

What is still needing work and attention?

Turn back to your Month 3 prompts on page 21-22. Read your responses of what was weighing you down. Have things changed since then? Are the same 'weights' (darkness, sin) still an issue? Why or why not?

**…God is light, and in him is no darkness at all.
If we say we have fellowship with him while we
walk in darkness, we lie and do not practice the
truth. But if we walk in the light, as he is in the
light, we have fellowship with one another and the
blood of Jesus his Son cleanses us from all sin.
1 John 1:5-7.**

Sin separates us from God. Walking in the darkness (sin) instead of with God (our Light), prevents us from drawing close to Him. Jesus Christ's death on the cross cleanses us from our sins and because of that, we can walk in the light. Are you walking in the light?

Journal what is holding you back from walking in the light in these dark areas of your life.

-Fear

-Anxiety

-Doubt

-Pride

Maybe fear, anxiety, doubt and pride aren't your areas of darkness? Write in your dark areas. Journal what is holding you back from the freedom and the light.

-_____

-_____

-_____

**Fear not, for I am with you; be not dismayed, for I
am your God; I will strengthen you, I will help you,
I will uphold you with my righteous right hand.
Isaiah 41:10**

How can you implement your One Word into these dark areas and begin walking in the light? What does that look like?

Spend time with God in prayer over this. Repent and confess your sins to Him. Ask the Spirit to lead you out of the dark and into the light. Ask God to remove the weight and burdens that have you trapped. Ask Him to help you automatically trust Him in these areas. Ask Him to comfort you and release you from holding onto these things. Journal your thoughts and prayers.

Work backwards. What steps can you take right now/today, to be out of the darkness and into the light in Month 12?

Use these next 3 months to work towards progress, instead of telling yourself you'll wait until next year. Make a 90 day plan to persevere on a new intention. This can be a small step, but make the step to move forward. You can do this. Consider using a tracker to chart your progress.

Optional Monthly Trackers

These monthly trackers are for your own use. Is God leading you to seek the light in a dark area of sin in your life? What small practice can you implement for the next 3 months? Write the activity name or practice, above each tracker and fill in the bubble each day you are successful.

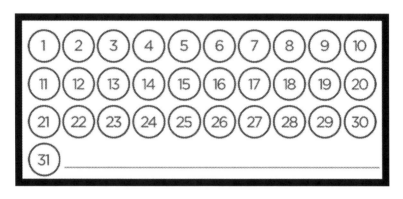

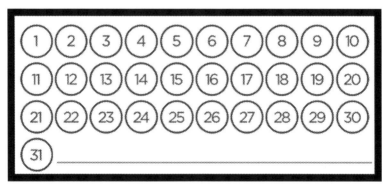

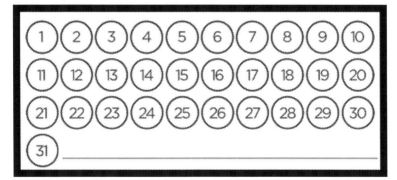

One Word Scripture Collection:

Choose another scripture to add to your One Word Scripture Collection. Maybe you'll want to add a light scripture or a do not fear scripture. Daily review your scripture collection and speak the verses aloud, pray these scriptures over yourself and allow the power of God's truths to soak into your soul, encourage you and equip you for the day.

Write out your scripture for the month in the box.

Optional Creative Activities:

Carve your One Word into a real or faux pumpkin or gourd and put it on display. You could also use decorative faux fruits and vegetables and add sticker letters to them as well. Place your vegetables in places that will catch your eye and remind you of your One Word intentions.

If interested, see page 141 for **More Creative Art Activities.**

Give Thanks Challenge:

**Every good gift and every perfect gift is from above,
coming down from the Father of lights with whom
there is no variation or shadow due to change.
James 1:17**

Continue to record the good and perfect gifts AND the not so perfect ones too. Trust the unchanging God to make good from all things. Keep going on this challenge and give Him thanks.

756.

757.

758.

759.

760.

761.

762.

763.

764.

765.

766.

767.

768.

769.

770.

771.

772.

773.

774.

775.

776.

777.

778.

779.

780.

781.

782.

783.

784.

785.

786.

787.

788.

789.

790.

791.

792.

793.

794.

795.

796.

797.

798.

799.

800.

801.

802.

803.

804.

805.

806.

807.

808.

809.

810.

811.

812.

813.

814.

815.

816.

817.

818.

819.

820.

821.

822.

823.

824.

825.

826.

827.

828.

829.

830.

831.

832.

833.

834.

835.

836.

837.

838.

839.

840.

MONTH 11 PROMPTS

But the fruit of the Spirit is love, joy, peace, patience, kindness, goodness, faithfulness, gentleness and self-control; against such things there is no law.
Galatians 5:22-23

Is your One Word a fruit of the Spirit? Yes or No?

Which fruits of the Spirit does your One Word most closely relate to?

Explain.

Think about your life and your current state of mind. How you are treating yourself and others? Rate yourself on which fruits are lacking from your 'diet' or life. 1 is barely showing up, 10 you have it down! Circle where you fall with each fruit.

Fruit of the Spirit	Low									High
Love	1	2	3	4	5	6	7	8	9	10
Joy	1	2	3	4	5	6	7	8	9	10
Peace	1	2	3	4	5	6	7	8	9	10
Patience	1	2	3	4	5	6	7	8	9	10

Kindness	1 2 3 4 5 6 7 8 9 10
Goodness	1 2 3 4 5 6 7 8 9 10
Faithfulness	1 2 3 4 5 6 7 8 9 10
Gentleness	1 2 3 4 5 6 7 8 9 10
Self-Control	1 2 3 4 5 6 7 8 9 10

Look back over your ranking and answer these questions:

Which fruits are strong in your life right now?

Are they showing strong to yourself?

Are they showing strong to others?

Are they strong in your spiritual life and relationship with God?

Explain.

Which fruits are lacking in your life right now?

Are they lacking to yourself?

Are they lacking to others?

Are they lacking in your spiritual life and relationship with God?

Explain.

Are you surprised at which fruits are strong and which are lacking?

Do they relate to your One Word? How?

Choose one fruit in each of the areas that you would like to intentionally focus on this month.

Fruit for myself_____

Fruit for others_____

Fruit in my spiritual life_____

How could you intentionally focus on these fruits in tandem with your One Word? Brainstorm ideas.

Can you set up a tracker this month and make some needed 'fruit' growth? Choose a small item or practice to start on this 'fruit growing' journey.

Optional Monthly Trackers

These monthly trackers are for your own use. Is God leading you to practice growing a fruit of the Spirit in your life? Write the activity name or practice above each tracker and fill in the bubble each day you are successful.

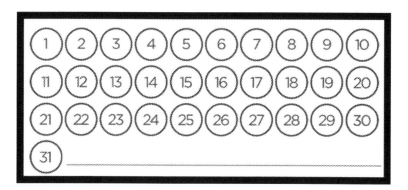

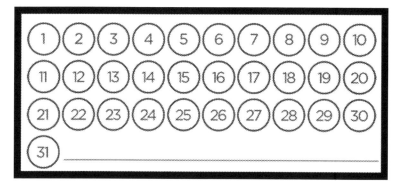

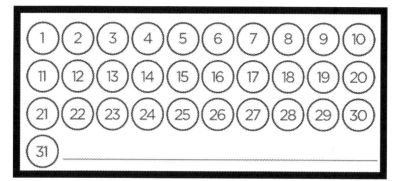

One Word Scripture Collection:

Choose another scripture to add to your One Word Scripture Collection or choose the Galatians 5:22-23 Fruits of the Spirit scripture. There's many children songs online to help you memorize this verse. Look for one to learn and memorize. Daily review your scripture collection and pray these scriptures over yourself.

Write out your scripture for the month in the box.

Optional Creative Activities:

Try writing a thankful letter to yourself, yes to you. Just like you were writing to encourage a friend, try encouraging yourself. Thank yourself, love on yourself, tell yourself what you are proud of and don't forget to tell yourself truths of who you are in Him. What do you need to hear and read right now? Try writing in the perspective of an 'older you' writing to your 'younger self'. Include a current picture of yourself to keep with the letter.

If interested, see page 141 for **More Creative Art Activities.**

LETTER TO MYSELF

Give Thanks Challenge:

**You will be enriched in every way to be
generous in every way, which through us
will produce thanksgiving to God.
2 Corinthians 9:11**

Give thanks with a grateful heart. Giving generously grows from having a thankful, grateful heart. Continue the Give Thanks Challenge of writing down all that you are thankful for.

841.

842.

843.

844.

845.

846.

847.

848.

849.

850.

851.

852.

853.

854.

855.

856.

857.

858.

859.

860.

861.

862.

863.

864.

865.

866.

867.

868.

869.

870.

871.

872.

873.

874.

875.

876.

877.

878.

879.

880.

881.

882.

883.

884.

885.

886.

887.

888.

889.

890.

891.

892.

893.

894.

895.

896.

897.

898.

899.

900.

901.

902.

903.

904.

905.

906.

907.

908.

909.

910.

124 |

911.

912.

913.

914.

915.

916.

917.

918.

919.

920.

921.

922.

923.

924.

MONTH 12 PROMPTS

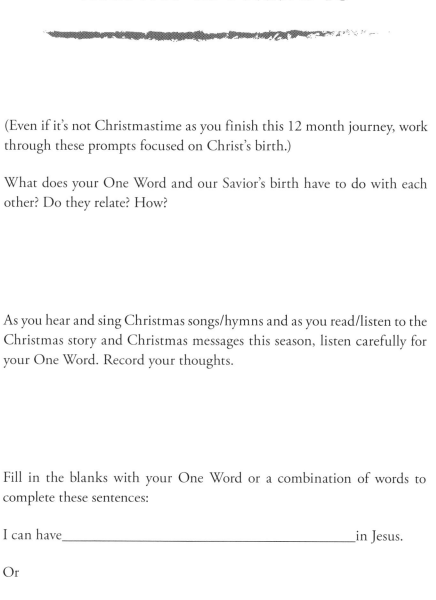

(Even if it's not Christmastime as you finish this 12 month journey, work through these prompts focused on Christ's birth.)

What does your One Word and our Savior's birth have to do with each other? Do they relate? How?

As you hear and sing Christmas songs/hymns and as you read/listen to the Christmas story and Christmas messages this season, listen carefully for your One Word. Record your thoughts.

Fill in the blanks with your One Word or a combination of words to complete these sentences:

I can have_____in Jesus.

Or

I can be_____in Jesus.

Because of Jesus, I can....

The all-powerful, redeeming love of Jesus Christ is for you. You can trust this. You can rely on this. You can live in freedom because of this. Once you have accepted the free gift of Jesus Christ as your Savior and God over your life, you instantly have the Holy Spirit within you. The Spirit is moving, working and guiding you to fulfill God's purposes for your life.

> **...**"**Repent and be baptized every one of you in the name of Jesus Christ for the forgiveness of your sins and you will receive the gift of the Holy Spirit.**"
> **Acts 2:38**

> **And hope does not put us to shame, because God's love has been poured into our hearts through the Holy Spirit who has been given to us.**
> **Romans 4:18**

Are you being called to repent?

Are you being called to be baptized?

How are you accessing the Holy Spirit right now? Or, how can you?

Start at the beginning of your journey and re-read when you first picked your One Word for the year. Read over all your entries from each month. Reread your manifesto. Reflect over your vision board. Reread all your scripture cards. Take some time to review these past 12 months.

How do you feel about your One Word now?

What do you want to remember about this journey?

What's one thing you must you never forget?

How has your faith grown because of your One Word? What changes do you notice about your faith?

Praise God for this year and the journey He has allowed you to have. Thank Him for guiding you throughout this year.

Optional Monthly Trackers

Is there any small practice you would like to track in this final month of your year-long journey? Write the activity name or practice above each tracker and fill in the bubble each day you are successful.

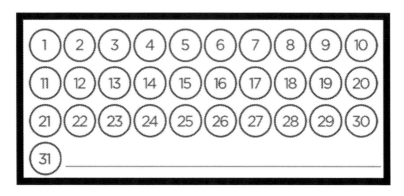

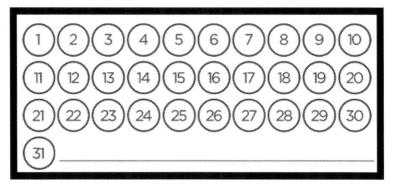

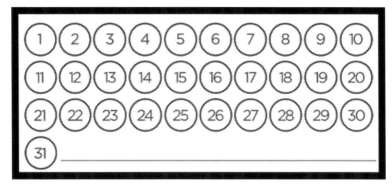

One Word Scripture Collection:

Choose one more scripture to add to your One Word Scripture Collection for the year. Review all your verses. Continue to keep your verses handy and practice memorizing them. Mark your year's collection with a colored ribbon or tag to remember this journey. If you choose to do this journey again, start a new scripture collection with a different color ribbon or marker, but don't forget to revisit your collection often. As you read through your verses, you'll remember your journey and growth.

Write out your scripture for the month in the box.

Optional Creative Activities:

Put your One Word on a Christmas tree ornament. This could easily be done by writing your One Word using a paint pen on a plain colored ornament. Other options to use are letter stickers, vinyl letters or even chalk and chalkboard paint. Tie a ribbon to the top, add an ornament hanger and display your One Word on your tree. Your ornament will be a special reminder to you of this journey. Even if Month 12 is not December, make a One Word ornament and tuck it away until Christmas.

If interested, see page 141 for **More Creative Art Activities.**

Give Thanks Challenge:

**"Amen! Blessing and glory and wisdom and
thanksgiving and honor and power and might
be to our God forever and ever! Amen."**
Revelation 7:12

Here it is! Complete this month's Give Thanks Challenge of recording your thankfulness to God and celebrate hitting 1000+ recorded gratitudes, but don't stop there…

925.

926.

927.

928.

929.

930.

931.

932.

933.

934.

935.

936.

937.

938.

939.

940.

941.

942.

943.

944.

945.

946.

947.

948.

949.

950.

951.

952.

953.

954.

955.

956.

957.

958.

959.

960.

961.

962.

963.

964.

965.

966.

967.

968.

969.

970.

971.

972.

973.

974.

975.

976.

977.

978.

979.

980.

981.

982.

983.

984.

985.

986.

987.

988.

989.

990.

991.

992.

993.

994.

995.

996.

997.

998.

999.

1000.

1001.

1002.

1003.

1004.

1005.

1006.

1007.

1008.

…whoa! Look at that, you did it! Over one thousand recorded thanksgivings. Why 1008 you ask? Each month you recorded 84 lines of gratitude. 84 x 12 months= 1008. You now have a few extra to finish the year out strong, but don't stop! You've established a wonderful habit and routine that happens when you give thanks. By doing this, you've taken your focus off yourself and your problems and have placed your focus on Him. You've been reminded that He's the giver of all good gifts and the one in control. You may have noticed that a heart of gratitude is a heart of joy that leaves no room for complaining and ungratefulness? Have you also noticed that when you praise and thank Him, you're trusting Him more and more? In other words, you've grown closer to Him just by giving Him thanks. Praise God! I encourage you to keep this practice up. Grab a blank journal or another copy of the One Word One Year Faith Journey and keep on thanking Him through another year and another.

ALL DONE, NOW WHAT?

Your work with your One Word will never be completely finished. Your chosen One Word is now a part of who you are. You'll still see it and remember it. It may appear in print and songs and your intentions from this past year will come to your mind all over again. Maybe you're excited to start a new 12 month journey with another One Word? That's great! You might find yourself being drawn to choose a new One Word that relates closely to your old One Word? That's OK and very common. Maybe you still have some unfinished work God wants to do in your life? Maybe you want to explore other aspects of your One Word?

Take time during this season to sit in stillness and be open to hearing from God. Is He directing you to another One Word for next year? Is a word reoccurring in your life and/or in your thoughts right now? What words are speaking to you? Write them down and ponder them. Ask God for direction. Be aware and open to what He may bring to your mind.

Is God leading you to start a One Word small group for the New Year? Who in your life could benefit from this practice and intentional focus? Could you commit to walking alongside a friend through this journey? Pray over this. Could this be an opportunity to mentor a friend in Christ?

Thank you for joining me on this One Word Faith Journey. I pray your year was filled with great spiritual growth, insights and a desire to continue seeking Him more and more. May you want to continue this journey again and again, year after year. Just pick up a new One Word One Year Faith Journey book and keep on going!

Love to you,
Michelle

SMALL GROUP ONE WORD FAITH JOURNEY

My favorite way to go through the One Word One Year Faith Journey is with a small group. There is no better way to provide encouragement, enthusiasm and accountability, than by being in a small group. Here are some suggestions if you would like to lead your own small group.

Gather 1 or more friends to complete the One Word One Year Faith Journey with you for the year. Ask for a year commitment to meet once a month. Order books for all members of your group.

Set a time, date, place for each monthly meeting. Do your best to be consistent and start and end on time. Plan for the group to meet for 1.5-2 hours at each meeting. (Once a month meetings work well, but feel free to do more than that.)

A week before each meeting, email the group members and remind them to work on their journal work for the month. It isn't mandatory that the journal prompts are done, but encourage the group members to spend a few minutes reading through and thinking about the prompts.

Each month decide ahead of time if a creative activity will take place during your meeting. If so, gather all supplies or ask members to bring supplies. If you are not a super creative person, ask another creative member to organize the activities for you. If needed, ask members to help reimburse for the cost of the supplies.

Organize your meeting agenda around the personalities of your group members. Some groups do better in conversation for the 1st hour, crafting the 2nd hour. Some groups like a creative outlet to warm up to conversation. Other groups may not want creative activities at all. Do what works.

At every meeting, lead the group into discussing some of the Monthly Prompts and sharing their monthly scriptures. Take turns listening and encouraging each other. Be sure that everyone has a chance to share. Remember to keep the focus on drawing near to God through their One Word.

As your group completes their year, encourage each member to start their own One Word small group for the next year. Ask your group members to pray over leading their own group and to be thinking of others who could benefit from this experience.

MORE CREATIVE ART ACTIVITIES

The process of creating art can calm your mind and soul as well as lower your stress level. Making One Word art not only provides a creative object to apply to your One Word, but when placed in your home you'll see it and be redirected to your intentions. The following activities are to inspire you to bring creative art to your One Word. These suggestions can also be used in your One Word small groups.

Paint your One Word on a rock. Look up rock verses to remind yourself that He is our solid foundation.

Design framed artwork with your One Word. Use paints, chalks or inks and create a visually pleasing modern backdrop. Apply your One Word to the art with letter stickers or vinyl letters and frame your art piece in a frame.

Paint or carve your One Word on a pumpkin or a gourd. Look up verses on God's provisions.

Make letter blocks with wood or paper to display your One Word. Spell out your One Word using letter art, stencils or paint. Put one letter on each block.

Make a paper, fabric or burlap banner that spells out your One Word. Craft a smaller sized banner that could hang across a wreath.

Design phone and/or computer screensavers that have your One Word on them.

Plant a flower or vegetable seedling and paint your One Word on a plant marker. As the plant grows, remind yourself of your spiritual growth.

Paint and 'bake' your One Word onto a mug or ceramic tiles for drink coasters.

Create jewelry and use metal stamps to personalize with your One Word.

Paint your one Word on a large seashell. Look up water and wave verses to remind yourself of His great love, power and control.

Assemble a scrapbook. Take pictures of your One Word in print or life. Develop photos and combine them into a small album or put on pages in this journal. Add scriptures as well.

Make subway art using your One Word and some of the synonyms of your One Word.

Decoupage your One Word to flower pots or other items in your home.

Write a poem or a song about your One Word.

Sew a quilt, bag, wall hanging, etc. with your One Word.

The possibilities are endless.

BOOKS READ

ACKNOWLEDGEMENTS

All praise to the Almighty God who allowed this book to be written, completed, published and used by many. You God, are my strength and I can do nothing without You.

Thank you to my husband Andy, who not only supported this adventure, but graciously edited my first draft and took out every single comma. Well, almost… I didn't let him edit my Acknowledgements page. Thank you to my children Jessica and Jacob. You are special gifts from God. I love you all so much.

Thank you to my mom, Pat Mooney and my dear church friend, Susan Boeker. Without you both asking for monthly prompts, this would have never become a curriculum.

Thank you to my prayer partners, Diane Bankson and Rebecca Posten. Diane introduced me to Lorrie Wilson, who graciously allowed me to take this faith-centered One Word concept and run with it. Thank you.

Thank you to my church home, Newport Covenant Church. Your continual support has encouraged me to grow in my faith and in my small group work in the church.

Thank you to my Ladies Bible Study members and leaders. You believed in me and never stopped loving me. What a gift you are.

And a huge thank you to my very first One Word small group. You showed up, supported my ideas and allowed me to witness God at work in you. I will treasure you always. Susan Boeker, Ellen Brenden, Heidi Goins, Carol Johnson, Angie Louie, Nicole Reeves and Linda Tjelle.

ABOUT THE AUTHOR

Michelle Paige Robblee, a former special education teacher, now leads women Bible studies and small discipleship groups at Newport Covenant Church in Bellevue, Washington. Happily married to Andy for over 25 years, they have 2 grown children and enjoy spending time together on Camano Island and traveling around the world. Michelle's passions extend to blogging her many creative ideas and parties at michellepaigeblogs.com.

Printed in the United States
By Bookmasters